TEN SUNS

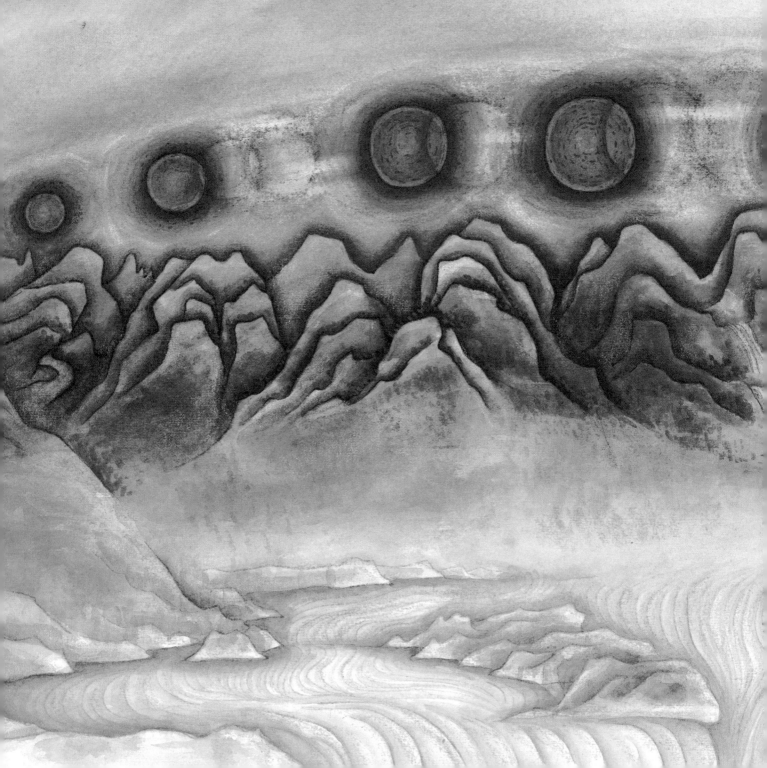

retold *by* ERIC A. KIMMEL

illustrated *by* YONGSHENG XUAN

TEN SUNS

A Chinese Legend

Holiday House/New York

Long ago, when the world was new, a giant mulberry tree grew on the far side of the sea, on the edge of the eastern horizon. Its roots plunged deep into the earth. Its branches scraped the sky.

Nestled in the topmost branches of this tree stood a jade palace. Hammered sheets of gold formed its roof. Its windows were made of the thinnest panes of amethyst and lapis lazuli. This was the palace of Di Jun, the eastern emperor, the god who ruled the regions of the sky where the sun arises.

In those days there were ten suns: the children of Di Jun
and his wife, Xi He. They never walked across the sky together. That would produce too much heat for the world to bear.
Instead, every morning before dawn, Xi He would awaken one
of her sons. They would climb into her dragon chariot and
drive to a point on the eastern horizon where Xi He's son
would begin his walk.

Each day one of the suns would walk across the sky from east to west. When the people on earth saw the sun crossing the heavens, bringing warmth and light, they offered thanks to Di Jun, Xi He, and their family.

But the gratitude of the earth's people and the importance of their work meant nothing to the boys. They found their task boring. Day after day, year after year, century after century, they followed the same path across the sky. There was no one to talk to, nothing new to see, nothing to do except follow that same weary track over and over again.

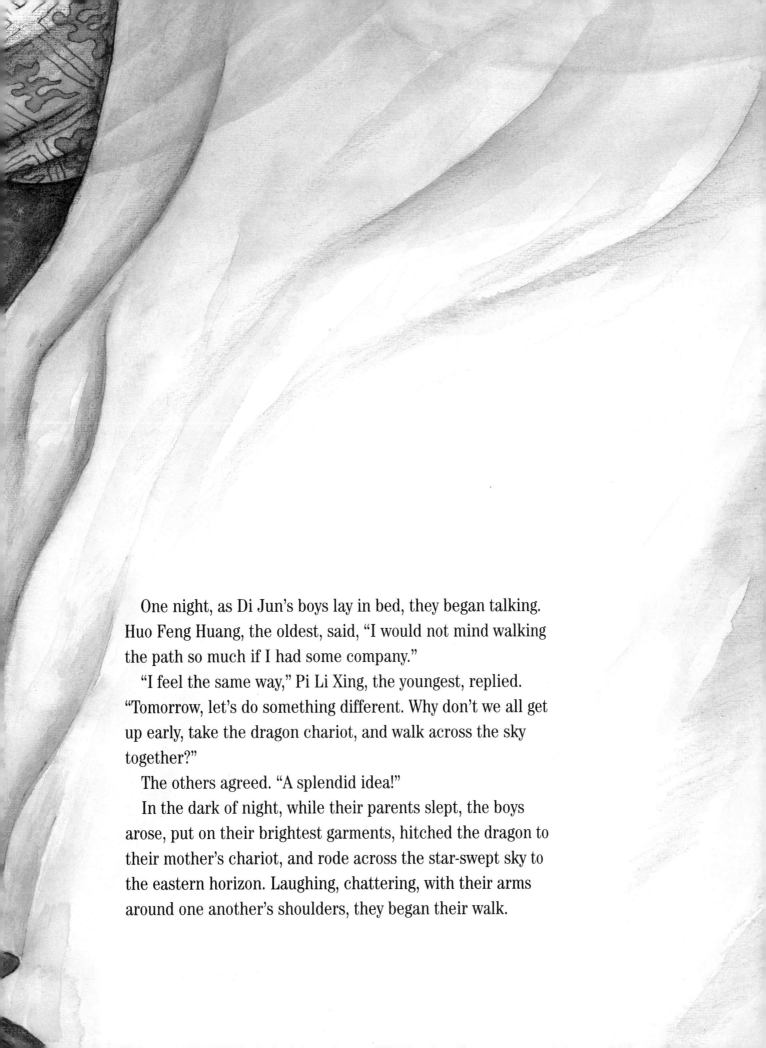

One night, as Di Jun's boys lay in bed, they began talking. Huo Feng Huang, the oldest, said, "I would not mind walking the path so much if I had some company."

"I feel the same way," Pi Li Xing, the youngest, replied. "Tomorrow, let's do something different. Why don't we all get up early, take the dragon chariot, and walk across the sky together?"

The others agreed. "A splendid idea!"

In the dark of night, while their parents slept, the boys arose, put on their brightest garments, hitched the dragon to their mother's chariot, and rode across the star-swept sky to the eastern horizon. Laughing, chattering, with their arms around one another's shoulders, they began their walk.

When dawn came, the people who lived on earth were astonished to see ten suns appear above the horizon. The blazing heat of ten suns shining down at once was more than the world could bear. Crops withered in the fields. Forests caught fire. Lakes and rivers dried up. Mountains shattered to pieces. The sea began to boil. People and animals grew faint. They stretched themselves on the scorching ground and waited to die.

The great emperor Shun, who ruled the nations of the world, cried to eastern god Di Jun.

"Why are you punishing us? What have the creatures of earth done to deserve this terrible fate? Have we not followed the proper rites? Have we not offered the correct sacrifices? Why have you sent your sons to destroy us?"

The great emperor's cries woke Di Jun and Xi He. They looked out the window of the jade palace. In the distance, they saw their ten sons marching together across the sky. Di Jun and Xi He called to them, "Come back at once! Go no further!"

But the boys did not listen. Earth was far below. They could not see the damage they were causing. Higher and higher they climbed, until they reached the place where the sun stands at noon.

Di Jun could not allow the world to be destroyed. The existence of all living things depended on him. If his sons would not abandon their reckless walk, he would have to stop them. Di Jun summoned Hu Yi, the Archer of Heaven.

Hu Yi had once been a man. He introduced the science of archery to the world by inventing the bow and arrow. As a reward for his discovery, the gods placed him in the heavens among the constellations.

Di Jun presented Hu Yi with a magic bow and ten magic arrows. With tears filling his eyes, he told Hu Yi, "Shoot down the ten suns—my sons—who are burning up the earth."

Hu Yi refused. "How can I harm your boys? They are like my children. I taught them to shoot with a bow and arrow. We both still love them, even when they disobey."

"I love the creatures of the earth, too. I must protect them," Di Jun told Hu Yi. "Do not be afraid. You will not harm the boys. My sons will not be hurt, but they will be changed. Never again will they cross the sky as suns. They will be gods no more. Hurry! Do as I command. There is no time to spare. The earth is dying."

Hu Yi took Di Jun's bow and magic arrows. He rode the wind down to earth. Taking his place on top of White Mountain, he planted his feet firmly and took careful aim. Hu Yi released the bowstring. The magic arrow streaked across the sky. It struck the first of the ten suns, shattering it to pieces.

One by one, Hu Yi's arrows found their mark. Each sun exploded, filling the sky with blinding light. The boys fell to earth, but they did not die. Instead, they turned into black-feathered birds. They became crows.

The emperor Shun watched the suns exploding in the sky. Suddenly he realized that if Hu Yi destroyed all the suns, there would be no heat or light. The earth would be plunged into icy darkness.

There was no time to spare. The emperor Shun summoned his fastest messenger.

"Go to the top of White Mountain. Find Hu Yi. Remove one arrow from his quiver to make sure he does not shoot down all the suns."

The messenger mounted his horse. He rode faster than he had ever ridden in his life, all the way to the top of White Mountain. There he saw Hu Yi. By now, only one sun remained in the sky. Shun's messenger plucked the last arrow from Hu Yi's quiver just as the Archer of Heaven reached for it. Finding no more magic arrows, Hu Yi assumed his work was done. He unstrung his bow and rode the wind back to the stars.

Since that day only one sun shines overhead. Every morning, the crows gather on White Mountain to greet the dawn. "*Gua! Gua!*" they call to their brother, the sun, as he begins his lonely walk across the sky.

For they remember that once they too were gods and hope for the day when their parents, Di Jun and Xi He, will forgive them.

AUTHOR'S NOTE

The story of the *Ten Suns* is one of the oldest Chinese myths, going as far back as the Shang dynasty (c. 1523 B.C.~1027 B.C.). There are several versions. The primary sources for this story were Anthony Christie's *Chinese Mythology* and Sandy Shepherd's *Myths and Legends from around the World.* YongSheng Xuan suggested names for Xi He's oldest and youngest sons. Pi Li Xing means Thunder Star. Hou Feng Huang means Phoenix Flame.

To Alison Sheridan-Herschede
E.A.K.

To Ken and Jean Mitchell
Y.S.X.

Library of Congress Cataloging-in-Publication Data

Kimmel, Eric A.
Ten suns: a Chinese legend / retold by Eric A. Kimmel;
illustrated by YongSheng Xuan. — 1st ed.
p.   cm.
Summary: When the ten sons of Di Jun walk across the sky together
causing the earth to burn from the blazing heat, their father looks
for a way to stop the destruction.
ISBN 0-8234-1317-9 (reinforced)
[1. Folklore—China.]   I. Xuan, YongSheng, ill.   II. Title.
PZ8.1.K567Te   1998
398.2'0951'01—DC21   96-30044   CIP   AC